McGraw-Hill

TRANSITIONS TO ENGLISH

McGraw-Hill School Division

New York   Oklahoma City   St. Louis   San Francisco   Dallas   Atlanta

Grateful acknowledgment for permission to reprint copy-righted material is made for:

Sizes from THE MAN WHO SANG THE SILLIES by John Ciardi. Copyright © 1961 by John Ciardi. Used by permission of Judith H. Ciardi, sole beneficiary of the estate of John Ciardi.

Little Chicken Forgets from CHICKEN FORGETS by Miska Miles. Text copyright © 1976 by Miska Miles. Reprinted by permission of Patrick J. Gallagher, Executor. Illustrated by Jim Arnosky. Copyright © 1976 by Jim Arnosky. Reprinted by permission of Susan Schulman Literary Agency, Inc.

Adaptation of *Lizzie and Harold* by Elizabeth Winthrop. Text copyright © 1986 by Elizabeth Winthrop. Reprinted by permission of Lothrop, Lee & Shepard Books (a division of William Morrow and Company, Inc.).

Down the Hill text and art excerpted from FROG AND TOAD ALL YEAR by Arnold Lobel. Copyright © 1976 by Arnold Lobel. Reprinted by permission of Harper & Row, Publishers, Inc.

I Have a Sister, My Sister Is Deaf from I HAVE A SISTER, MY SISTER IS DEAF written by Jeanne Whitehouse Peterson, illustrated by Deborah Kay. Text copyright © 1977 by Jeanne Whitehouse Peterson. Illustration copyright © 1977 by Deborah Ray. Reprinted by permission of Harper & Row, Publishers, Inc.

Farming from PARTNERS by Betty Baker. Copyright © 1978 by Betty Baker. Reprinted by permission of the author's representative.

Adaptation of *The Best New Thing* by Isaac Asimov. Text copyright © 1971 by Isaac Asimov. Reprinted by permission of Philomel Books.

What Is That Alligator Saying? from WHAT IS THAT ALLIGATOR SAYING? by Ruth Belov Gross. Copyright © 1972 by Ruth Belov Gross. Reprinted by permission of Scholastic, Inc.

The Whale Of Whales from ONE WINTER NIGHT IN AUGUST by X. J. Kennedy. Copyright © 1975 by X. J. Kennedy. Reprinted by permission of Curtis Brown, Ltd.

Alexander and the Wind-up Mouse from ALEXANDER AND THE WIND-UP MOUSE by Leo Lionni. Copyright © 1969 by Leo Lionni. Reprinted by permission of Pantheon Books, a division of Random House, Inc.

Illustration
Jim Arnosky 20-27; Ned Delaney 56-67; Nancy Didion 92-99; Julie Durrell 36-45; Linda Edwards 100-109; Tom Garcia 10; Dennis Hockerman 110-119; Leo Lionni 148-162; Arnold Lobel 68-77; Susan Miller 12-19; Leslie Morrill 46-55, 128-135; John O'Brien 1-9; Jan Pyk 136; Deborah Kogan Ray 78, 80, 81-82, 84, 86, 87-88; Karen Schmidt 174; Jerry Smath 120-126; Mary Szilagyi 28-35.

Photography
David Kramer 90; J. C. Carton/Bruce Coleman, Inc. 129; Bruce Coleman, Inc. 130; E. R. Degginger/Animals, Animals 131; Ted Levin/Animals, Animals 132; S. J. Kraseman/Peter Arnold, Inc. 133; Courtesy of Random House 165.

ISBN 0-07-016617-X

McGraw-Hill Publishing
1200 Northwest 63rd Street
Oklahoma City, Oklahoma 73116-5712

890-8976

TRANSITIONS TO ENGLISH

Table of Contents ◆

Unit 1: Sizes/Big and Little

Unit 2: Family and Friends

Unit 3: Places

Unit 4: Animals

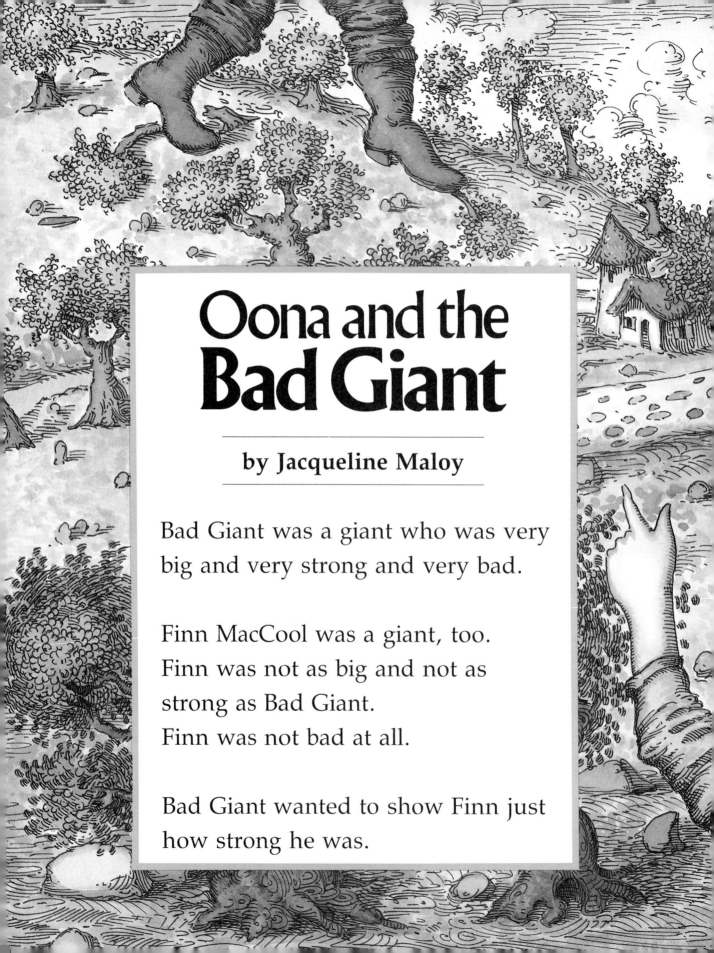

Oona and the Bad Giant

by Jacqueline Maloy

Bad Giant was a giant who was very big and very strong and very bad.

Finn MacCool was a giant, too. Finn was not as big and not as strong as Bad Giant. Finn was not bad at all.

Bad Giant wanted to show Finn just how strong he was.

Finn MacCool had a wife named Oona.
She could hear very well.

"Bad Giant wants to see
you," said Oona to Finn.
"I can hear him."

"What can I do?" said Finn.
"I do not have time to run away."

"Do not run away," said Oona.
"I can take care of him."
Oona made a rock look like a cake.

1

Then she put a baby's hat on Finn.
She made him sit in a baby's bed.

"Stay there," she said.
"Bad Giant will think you are a baby.
I will take care of Bad Giant.
Can you tell me why Bad Giant is
so big and strong?"

"Bad Giant is big and strong because
he has a big ring," said Finn.

Bad Giant came to the house.

"I am looking for Finn MacCool,"
said Bad Giant.

"Finn is not home," said Oona.
"I am Finn's wife.
This is Finn's baby.
We are waiting for Finn to get back.
He is away, looking for a giant named
Bad Giant."

3

"I am Bad Giant," said Bad Giant.
"I will wait for him."

Bad Giant looked at Finn in the
baby's bed.
"That is a very big baby," he said.

"Yes, but he is not as big as
Finn MacCool," said Oona.

"He is not as big and strong as I am,"
said Bad Giant.

"You do look strong," said Oona.
"Can you take me and the baby to the
lake for a drink?"

"Get on my back," said Bad Giant.
"I will take you and the baby to
the lake."

"Finn can do better than that.
He brings the house with us.
The baby and I ride in the house.
Can you do that?" said Oona.

5

"If Finn can do it, so can I," Bad
Giant said.
Bad Giant took the house to the lake.
Then he put it down very fast.

"There," he said, "I can do what
Finn MacCool can do."

"That was very good," said Oona.
"Take this good cake that I made.
Finn and the baby like this cake."

6

It was the rock that looked like a
cake.
Bad Giant could not eat it.
"Who can eat a cake like this?"
he said.

"Why, Finn and the baby can eat
cakes like this," said Oona.
"See, the baby wants more."

Finn, in the baby's hat, was eating
a cake that was not made of rocks.

"How can a baby eat this cake?" said Bad Giant.

Then he went to look at Finn.

"Grab the ring!" said Oona.

"I have it!" said Finn MacCool.

"Now I will not be as big and strong as I was," said Bad Giant.

"You took good care of me, Oona," said Finn.

"I took care of Bad Giant, too," said Oona.

- ◆ **Think** How did Oona take good care of Finn?

- ◆ **Share** Find a part of the story that you think is funny. Read it to the class.

- ◆ **Write** Write a sentence. Tell what you liked best about Oona's big plan to help Finn.

Sizes

If you were as big as a giant flea,
How much would you have to
grow to be
The size of the tiniest head-to-tail
Very most midgety baby whale?

I mean to say—and it's no surprise—
Whatever you do about your size,
There's always something a size or two
Very much bigger or smaller than you.

I mean to say, what's big of some
Is small of others. Now get along
home.
And whether you stay or wander far,
Be just the size of whatever you are.

John Ciardi

10

◆ **Think**   What is the smallest thing in the poem? What is the largest thing?

◆ **Share**   What other "giant" things do you know? What other "tiniest" things do you know? Share your big and little things with the class.

◆ **Write**   Write a new last line for the poem. Be sure to use a word that rhymes with are.

The Brave Tailor

by Dinah Anastasio

There was a tailor in Little Town.
One day, this tailor wanted cake.
There were many flies on the cake.

"Get away from my cake, flies,"
he said.
The tailor hit the flies.

"I got seven flies," he said.
"I want all the people in Big Town to
know about this!"

The tailor made a big belt that
said, "Seven at One Time."
He went to Big Town.
The people in Big Town saw the belt.

"He got seven at one time, but seven
what?" said a woman.
The people did not think of flies.

"We will take the tailor to the queen.
The queen will know how to get rid of
this tailor," said a man.

13

The people took the tailor to the queen.

The queen said, "Brave tailor, you
have scared the people in Big Town.
They want me to get rid of you.
But you can stay if you help us.
There are seven bad giants who just
moved to Big Town.
We do not want to let bad giants stay
in Big Town.
Get rid of the seven bad giants!
Then you can stay in Big Town."

"I will do that," said the tailor.
"I am not scared.
To get rid of the seven giants
I will need two things.
Let me have an egg and a bird."

The queen got an egg and a bird for
the tailor.
The tailor took the egg and the bird
from the queen.
Then he went to find the seven
giants.

The tailor found the seven giants.
The giants looked down and saw the
little tailor's belt.

"So, you got seven at one time," one
giant said to the tailor.

The tailor said, "Yes I did.
I can get you, too!"

"You can, can you?" said the giant.

16

The biggest giant got a rock and broke
it with a big club.

"I can do better than that," said the
tailor.
"I can do that with one hand."

The tailor took the egg and broke it.
The giants did not see that it was an egg.

"You broke a rock," said a giant.

Then a giant got a little rock.

"You are strong, but can you throw a rock like I can?" he said.
The rock went up in the sky and came down.

"I can do better than that," said the tailor.
He took the bird in one hand and let it go.
The bird went up and up and up.

18

"A man that strong can get seven of us at a time!" said the scared giants. They ran away from the tailor.

The queen was glad to be rid of the giants.
The little tailor was glad, too.

- ◆ **Think** What did people think of the tailor when they saw the belt?

- ◆ **Share** What do you think was the best thing the tailor did?

- ◆ **Write** Write a sentence. Tell about something you can do.

Chicken Forgets

by Miska Miles

"Chicken," the mother hen said,
"I need your help.
I need a basket of wild berries."

"I would like to get berries," the
little chicken said.

"Take this basket and fill it to the
top," the mother hen said.
"Sometimes you forget things.
THIS time, please, please don't
forget the berries."

"I will not forget," the little
chicken said.
Because he didn't want to forget,
he said over and over, "Get wild
berries.
Get wild berries."

All the way to the lake he said,
"Get wild berries."

Then the chicken saw a frog.

"What are you saying?" the frog said.

"Get wild berries," the chicken said.

"Don't say that to me," the frog said.

"What do you want me to say?" said
the chicken.

"Get a big green fly," the frog said.

The chicken went on his way.
And because he didn't want to forget,
he said, "Get a big green fly.
Get a big green fly."

All the way to the farm, the chicken said, "Get a big green fly."

"Don't say that to me," a goat said.

"What do you want me to say?" said the chicken.

"Get green weeds," said the goat.

And on the chicken went, saying, "Get green weeds.
Get green weeds."

"No, no," said a robin.
"Berries are better.
Follow me.
I will show you the place."

So the little chicken ran in the
grass, following the robin.
The chicken came to a place where
there were many wild berries.

The robin ate and ate and ate.

And the little chicken filled his basket
with wild berries.

He went on his way home.
Back he went, by the farm and by
the lake.
He ate five berries.

Across the grass, he went.
And he ate three berries.

At home, the mother hen looked at
the basket.

"You DIDN'T forget," the mother
hen said.
"You did bring home berries and the
basket is just about filled to the top.
You are a good little chicken.
I am so glad."

And the little chicken was glad, too.

♦ **Think**   Did the little chicken forget?

♦ **Share**   Did the frog and the goat help the little chicken?

♦ **Write**   Make a list. Write two things to do when you do not want to forget something.

Jill and the New Baby

by Maggie Palmer

"Your mother is bringing home
your new baby sister today," said
Grandpa to Jill.

"Now I will not be the baby.
I don't like being older," said
Jill.
She felt a little sad.

"Your mother will need you to help
care for your new baby sister,"
Grandpa said.

"What can I do to help Mother?"
said Jill.
"I am too little to help."

"You were too little, but you are
older now," said Grandpa.
"There are so many things you
can do.
You can help me now if you like."

Jill went with Grandpa to the shop.
Grandpa made things with wood in
the shop.

This was the very first time that
Grandpa had wanted Jill to help
him make something.

"But I am too little to help you
in your shop," said Jill.
"You said that I was."

"Yes, I did," said Grandpa.
"But you are older now."

Grandpa showed Jill a nice new
bed made of wood.

"I made this bed for your sister,"
said Grandpa.
"But I think it needs one more
thing.
What do you think?"

Jill looked at the bed.
It was a very nice little bed made
of new wood.
She saw the one thing that
it needed.

"It needs to be painted," she said.

"Yes," said Grandpa.
"Will you help me paint it?"

Jill helped Grandpa to paint the bed.
They painted it blue.
When the bed was painted, Grandpa
looked at it.

"It still needs one more thing,"
he said.
"What do you think it needs,
Jill?"

Jill looked at the little bed.
She saw what it needed.
Jill got red paint.

"What are you going to paint,
Jill?" said Grandpa.

"You will see," said Jill.

She painted big red trucks on
the bed.

"Isn't this nice?" said Jill.

"It looks very nice.
I like the trucks best of all.
I think your new little sister is
going to like it," said Grandpa.

Jill felt glad.
She liked to think about the
little baby sleeping in the bed.

"Are you still sad that you are
the older sister?" said Grandpa.

"No," said Jill.
"Now that I am older, maybe I
can do more things with you.
I can help with my new sister.
It is nice to get older."

◆ **Think** How did Grandpa help
change the way Jill felt about
the new baby?

◆ **Share** What helped Jill be glad
about her new sister?

◆ **Write** Write a list. Tell two
ways you could help a new baby.

A Nice Little Gift

by Noel Celsi

Maria wanted to get Mother a gift.
She went to talk to Sam about it.

"Where can I get a good gift for
my mother?" she asked Sam.

"Your mother likes plants," said Sam.
"Why don't you get your mother a
little plant at the plant store?"

Maria went to the plant store and
got a plant.
She gave the plant to Mother.

"What a nice plant!" said Mother,
when she saw it.
"And what a good gift!
Would you help me take care of
the plant, Maria?" she asked.

"Yes, I would," said Maria.

"If we take good care of this plant
it will grow," Mother said.

Maria and Mother took care
of the plant, but it did not
grow at all.

"Why isn't it growing?" asked
Maria at last.
"Isn't it well?"

"I don't know," said Mother.
She looked at the plant.

38

"There are things we can do to help the plant grow," Mother said.

First, they took the plant and moved it to a place in the sun.

"A plant needs sun to grow," said Mother.

The plant stayed in the sun for many days, but it did not grow at all.

"Now what can we do?" asked Maria.

Mother said, "A plant needs to be
watered.
Maybe if we water it more, it will
grow."

So Mother watered the plant.
Still, the plant did not grow.

At last Mother said, "There is one
more thing to try.
The plant is in a very little pot.
We will go back to the plant store
and get a big pot.
Maybe then the plant will grow."

They went back to the plant store.
They found a big pot in the store and
took it home.
They put the plant in the big pot,
watered it, and put it in the sun.

Then the plant did grow!
How the plant did grow!

"This plant looks like it will grow into
a tree!" said Maria.

She and Mother looked at the plant.

"That plant is too big for the house,"
said Mother.
"We cannot have a plant that big
in this little house.
What can we do?"

43

"It was a nice little plant when
you gave it to me," said Mother.
"Now look at it!"

"I know what we can do," said Maria.
"We can cut pieces from the plant.
The pieces will make new little plants.
The little plants will make nice
gifts for everyone we know."

44

And that is what they did.
They cut little pieces from
the big plant.
Next, they gave the little pieces
away as gifts.
Everyone who got a piece of the plant
was glad to get a nice little gift.

◆ **Think** What made Maria's gift
grow?

◆ **Share** What could Maria do if the
plant got big again?

◆ **Write** Write a sentence. Tell about
a good gift that you can make.

The Winter Sleep

by John Maloy

Tim Rabbit had a home in the woods.
It was nice there when it was warm.
He could find all the food he wanted
to eat.
It was fun to play in the grass.
But every winter, it was not so nice in
the woods.
There was ice on the grass.
There was very little food, and it was
very cold.

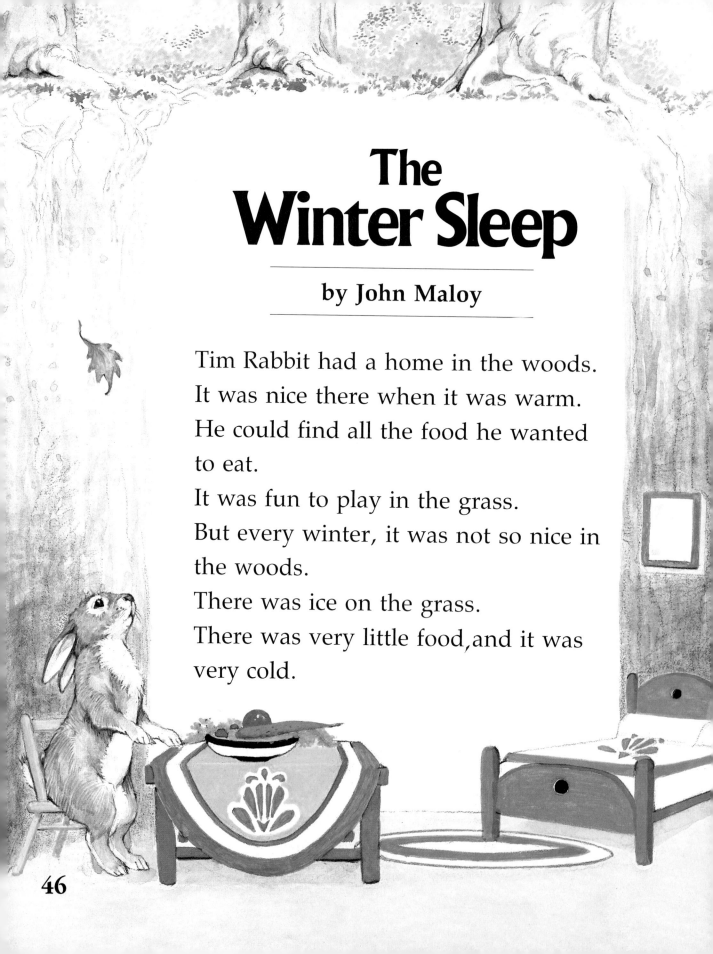

46

One day, Tim Rabbit saw Max Bear.
Tim Rabbit said, "My friends and I
don't like the winter.
There is all that ice, and we cannot
find food."

Max Bear said, "I like winter.
When it gets cold, I eat more food.
Then I go into my warm home and I
sleep all winter."

This made Tim Rabbit think.

Tim Rabbit went to see Fran Rabbit.
Tim Rabbit said, "Bears have a good
time every winter.
They sleep."

"I wish we could sleep every winter,
too," said Fran Rabbit.

Tim and Fran Rabbit went to talk to
Max Bear.

Max Bear said, "I would be glad to let you sleep at my house all winter. I will tell you what we must do to have a good sleep.
First, we must get very tired."

"How will we get tired?" asked Fran Rabbit.

Max Bear said, "One way to get tired is to run fast."

"We do not run," said Tim Rabbit. "We hop."

So, Tim and Fran hopped around and around the woods, but they did not get tired.

Max Bear said, "Maybe it would help if you found something dull to do."

Fran said, "We can go see Nat Turtle!"

50

Max Bear said, "Nat Turtle could make
a rock yawn."

So Fran and Tim went to see Nat Turtle.
The plan worked.
Nat Turtle could not stop telling
dull stories.

Soon Tim and Fran Rabbit got tired.
They yawned and said goodnight, but
Nat Turtle went on telling dull stories
to the trees.

Back at home, Max Bear had food and
warm drinks for Tim and Fran.
He ran around singing a song.
He was so glad to have friends come
to stay with him.

In the woods, it got very cold.
But Max's home was nice and warm,
just as Max had said it would be.
Tim and Fran Rabbit were telling
bedtime stories.

For a time, Max Bear was scared
that Tim and Fran Rabbit would not
get to sleep.

Max said, "I would be glad to show
you my home movies."

But Tim and Fran did not think that
movies would be fun.

Max sang a bedtime song.
Tim and Fran yawned and yawned.
They all fell into a good sleep.

Tim and Fran got up.
Max Bear was still sleeping.
It was still winter.

"What can we do?" asked Fran.

"Maybe we could look at the home
movies now," Tim said to Fran.

Tim and Fran stayed in Max's house
all winter.
At night they went to sleep.
Every day they looked at movies.
They had a good winter.

♦ **Think** Why did Tim and Fran want
to stay with Max all winter?

♦ **Share** What do you think the
rabbits will do when it gets warm?

♦ **Write** Write a sentence. Tell what
you can do to help you go to sleep.

Lizzie and Harold

by Elizabeth Winthrop

Lizzie wanted a best friend right away.
"Today I am going to find my best
friend," Lizzie told Harold.

Harold lived next door.
Every day they walked to school
together.

"Why do you want a best friend?"
Harold asked.

"Because I need someone to tell
secrets to and I want someone who
likes me as much as I like her,"
Lizzie said.

"I will be your best friend,"
Harold said.

"You can't be," Lizzie said.
"You are a boy."

"So what?" said Harold.
Lizzie did not answer.

The next day Lizzie wore a pink
flowered dress and black party shoes
to school.

"You look funny," Harold said.

"I look like Christina," Lizzie answered.
"She is going to be my new best friend."

"I like you best when you look like Lizzie," Harold said.

When Lizzie got to school, she ran up to Christina.

"I am wearing a dress and party shoes
just like you," said Lizzie.
"I want you to be my best friend."

"I don't want a best friend,"
Christina said.

"You don't?" said Lizzie.

"No," said Christina.
She walked away.

"How is your new friend?" Harold
asked on the way home.

"Don't ask," said Lizzie.
"Christina is not my best friend
after all."

"That was quick," said Harold.

The next day, Lizzie put a sign on the
door of her house.
The doorbell rang.
Lizzie ran to open it.

There stood Harold.

"Here I am," he said.
"Your new best friend."

"You can't be my best friend," Lizzie
said.
"You are a boy."

Nobody else rang the doorbell.
Lizzie took down the sign.

61

"Does that mean that I am your best friend now?" Harold asked.

"No," said Lizzie.
"That means I give up.
I don't want a best friend after all."

The next day Harold was carrying a big blue bag to school.

"What is in your bag?" asked Lizzie.

"It is my trick-or-treat candy," said Harold.

"Why are you taking it to school?"
asked Lizzie.

"I am going to give it to the person
who promises to be my best friend,"
said Harold.
"Since you don't want to be my best
friend, I am going to find somebody
else."

"Harold, you can't find a best friend
that way," Lizzie said.

"Why not?" asked Harold.

"Because best friends just happen to you.
Besides, I thought you wanted to be my best friend!" Lizzie cried.

But Harold wasn't listening.

All day long Lizzie thought about Harold.
When she met him after school, he did not have his blue bag of candy.

"I have a new best friend," Harold
said.
"He is a boy.
He ate all my candy and his name is
Douglas."

"Why do you look so sad?" Lizzie
asked.

"Because I like you better," said Harold.

"Well, I have a new best friend, too,"
Lizzie said.
"He is a boy.
He likes me as much as I like him."

Harold looked even sadder.
"What is his name?" Harold asked.

"Harold," said Lizzie.

After You Read

Think

1. Why didn't Lizzie want Harold as a best friend at first?

2. What did Lizzie and Harold do to try to get best friends?

3. Who did Lizzie's best friend turn out to be?

Share

What makes a friend your best friend?

Write

Write an ending for the sentence, *You know someone is your best friend when* ____.

Read

Read more about good friends in ''George and Martha, What Do You See?'' by James Marshall.

Down the Hill

by Arnold Lobel

Frog went to Toad's house.

"Toad, wake up!" Frog cried.
"Come out and see how great the
winter is."

"I will not," said Toad.
"I am in my warm bed."

"Winter is great," said Frog.
"Come out and have fun."

"No," said Toad.
"I have no winter clothes."

Frog came into the house.
"I have some clothes for you to put
on," he said.

Frog pulled a coat down over the top
of Toad.
Frog pulled pants up over Toad's
feet and legs.
He put a hat upon Toad's head.

"Help!" cried Toad.
"My best friend is trying to kill me
with a coat, pants, and a hat!"

"I am just getting you ready for
winter," laughed Frog.

Frog and Toad went out.
They tramped in the snow.

"We will ride down this big hill
upon my sled," said Frog.

"Not me," said Toad.

"Do not be afraid," said Frog.
"I will be with you on the sled.
It will be a fine, fast ride.
Toad, you sit in front.
I will sit right behind you."

Frog sat behind Toad on the sled.
The sled moved down the hill.

"Are you ready?
Here we go!" said Frog.

There was a bump.
Frog fell off the sled.
Toad rushed past trees and rocks.

"Frog, I am glad that you are here,"
said Toad.
"I would not like to be by myself."

Toad leaped over a hill of snow.
"I could not drive the sled without
you behind me," said Toad.
"You are right.
Winter is great!" he laughed.

A bird was flying by.

"Look at Frog and me," called Toad.
"We can ride a sled better than
everyone in the world!"

"But Toad," said the bird.
"Frog is not on the sled."

Toad looked behind him.
He saw that Frog was not there.

"I AM ALL BY MYSELF!" cried Toad.

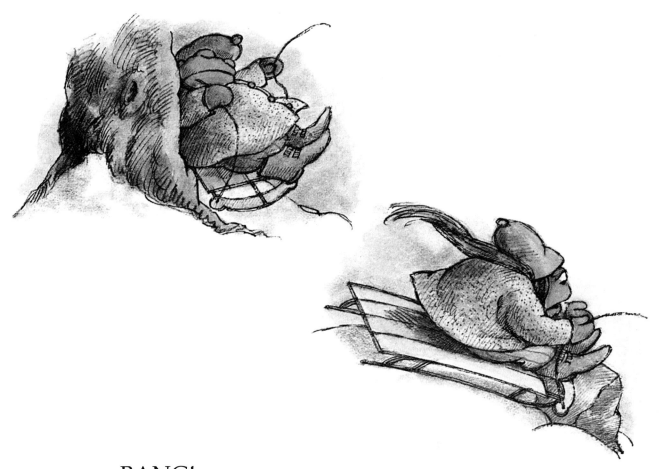

BANG!
The sled hit a tree.

THUD!
The sled hit a rock.

PLOP!
The sled went right into the snow.

Frog came running down the hill.
He pulled Toad out of the snow.

"I saw everything," said Frog.
"You did very well without me."

"I did not," said Toad.
"But there is one thing that I am
ready to do all by myself."

"What is that?" asked Frog.

"I can go home by myself," said Toad.
"I quit.
It may be true that winter is great,
but bed is better."

After You Read

Think

1. What do Frog and Toad think about winter?

2. Can Toad ride a sled well?

3. Why do you think Toad likes the sled ride at first, but not at the end?

Share

What did Toad learn about winter?

Write

Write a list.
List the things you like to do best in winter.

Read

You can read more about winter in "The Snowy Day" by Ezra Jack Keats.

How would you tell about someone you know very well? In this story, a girl tells about her sister and the things they do together.

I Have a Sister
My Sister Is Deaf

by Jeanne Whitehouse Peterson

I have a sister. My sister is deaf. She is special. There are not many sisters like mine.

My sister can play the piano. She likes to feel the deep rumbling chords. But she will never be able to sing. She cannot hear the tune.

My sister can dance with a partner or march in a line. She likes to leap, to tumble, to roll, to climb to the top of the monkey bars.

She watches me as we climb. I watch her, too. She cannot hear me shout, "Look out!" But she can see me swinging her way. She laughs and swings backward, trying to catch my legs.

I have a sister who likes to go with me out to the grassy lot behind our house. Today we are stalking deer. I turn to speak to her. I use no voice, just my fingers and my lips. She understands and walks behind me, stepping where I step.

I am the one who listens for small sounds. She is the one who watches for quick movements in the grass.

When my sister was very small, when I went to school and she did not, my sister learned to say some words. Each day she sat on the floor with our mother, playing with some toys we keep in an old shoe box. "It's a ball," our mother would say. "It's a dog. It's a book."

When I came home, I also sat on the floor. My sister put her hands into the box. She smiled and said, "Ball."

Baaaa! it sounded to me. "It's a ball," I repeated, just like our mother did.

My sister nodded and smiled. "Ball," she said once more. Again it sounded like *baaaa!* to me.

Now my sister has started going to my school, although our mother still helps her speak and lip-read at home. The teacher and children do not understand every word she says, like *sister* or *water* or *thumb*. Today the children in her room told me, "Your sister said *blue!*"

Well, I heard her say that a long time ago. But they have not lived with my sister for five years the way I have.

I understand my sister. My sister understands what I say too, especially if I speak slowly and move my hands a lot. But it is not only my lips and fingers that my sister watches.

I wore my sunglasses yesterday. The frames are very large. The lenses are very black. My sister made me take them off when I spoke. What do my brown eyes say to her brown eyes? That I would really rather play ball than play house? That I just heard our mother call, but I do not want to go in yet?

Yes, I have a sister who can understand what I say. But not always. Last night I asked, "Where are my pajamas?" She went into the kitchen and brought out a bunch of bananas from the fruit bowl on the table.

My friends ask me about my little sister. They ask, "Does it hurt to be deaf?" "No," I say, "her ears don't hurt, but her feelings do when people do not understand."

My sister cannot always tell me with words what she feels. Sometimes she cannot even show me with her hands. But when she is angry or happy or sad, my sister can say more with her face and shoulders than anyone else I know.

I tell my friends I have a sister who knows when a dog is barking near her and who says she does not like the feel of that sound. She knows when our cat is purring if it is sitting on her lap, or that our radio is playing if she is touching it with her hand.

But my sister will never know if the telephone is ringing or if someone is knocking at the door. She will never hear the garbage cans clanging around in the street.

I have a sister who sometimes cries at night, when it is dark and there is no light in the hall. When I try plugging my ears in the dark, I cannot hear the clock ticking on the shelf or the television playing in the living room. I do not hear any cars moving out on the street. There is nothing. Then I wonder, is it the same?

I have a sister who will never hear the branches scraping against the window of our room. She will not hear the soft music of the wind chimes I have hung up there. But when the storms come, my sister does not wake to the sudden rolling thunder, or to the quick clap-clap of the shutters in the wind. My little sister sleeps. I am the one who is afraid.

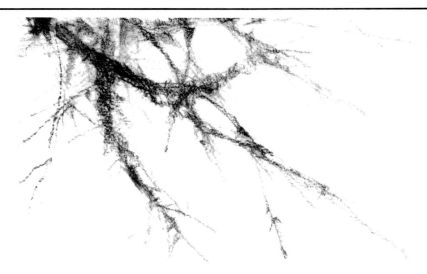

When my friends ask, I tell them I have a sister who watches television without turning on the sound. I have a sister who rocks her dolls without singing any tune. I have a sister who can talk with her fingers or in a hoarse, gentle voice. But sometimes she yells so loud, our mother says the neighbors will complain.

I stamp my foot to get my sister's attention, or wave at her across the room. I come up behind her and put my hand on her arm. She can feel the stamping. She can feel the touching. She can see my moving hand from the corner of her eye. But if I walk up behind her and call out her name, she cannot hear me.

I have a sister.

My sister is deaf.

A Reader Says

*I think these two sisters had fun together. I wish
I had a sister.*

How did you feel about the story?

After You Read

Think

1. How does the sister who is deaf let others know how she feels?
2. How does the sister who is deaf know what people are saying or feeling?
3. How does the older sister feel about having a sister who is deaf?
4. What do you think are the nicest things the sisters did for each other?

Share

Tell which of the sisters in the story you would like to meet. Why? Share your ideas. Then listen as others tell which sister they would like to meet and why.

Write

Write a letter to the sister you would like to meet. Tell the sister you choose what you would like to do together.

About the Author

Jeanne Whitehouse Peterson

Jeanne Whitehouse Peterson really has a sister who is deaf. When Mrs. Peterson started writing, she wrote about growing up with her sister. "That's what I knew best," she explains. "I wanted to share the joys and sorrows of the deaf child."

Mrs. Peterson was born in Walla Walla, Washington. When she was twelve, she wrote stories in her uncle's barn. Then she fed the pages to the cows! She is now a schoolteacher as well as a writer. She lives in Albuquerque, New Mexico. She likes reading stories out loud. She also likes hearing others read out loud to her. Some of Peterson's other books are *That Is That* and *While the Moon Shines Bright*.

City Magic

**by Laura Schenone
and Pat Garbarini**

I want a pet very, very much.
My mother says I have to wait.
We have had this talk many times,
my mother and I.
Dad says I can buy some fish.
They are small and can fit well in
my small room.
But my brother has four fish.
I want something different.
I want something of my own.

One day, Grandma showed me
flowers hanging in her window.
She had many kinds of flowers.
Grandma told me she would help me
grow flowers of my own.
She said that they are not the same
as a pet, but that flowers can
bring magic to a city home.

Grandma took me to buy some flower
seeds and told me what to do.
Now I have all kinds of flowers
hanging in the window of my room.
I still want a pet, but a window
full of flowers is nice, too.

How to Grow a Flower

There are many different kinds
of flowers that are easy to grow.
Most flowers can be started as seeds.
Here is an easy way to grow a flower
from a seed.

To grow a flower, you will need
to do these things:

- ◆ buy your seeds
- ◆ buy or make a pot
- ◆ get some soil
- ◆ get three or four small rocks
- ◆ get some water.

1. Get a small pot for your flower.
   You can use a can for a pot.
   Clean the can out very well.
   Get someone to help you make
   three or four small holes in the
   end of the can.

2. Put the rocks in the pot.
   They will help to keep the soil
   from being too wet.

3. Fill the pot with soil so that
   it is not quite full.

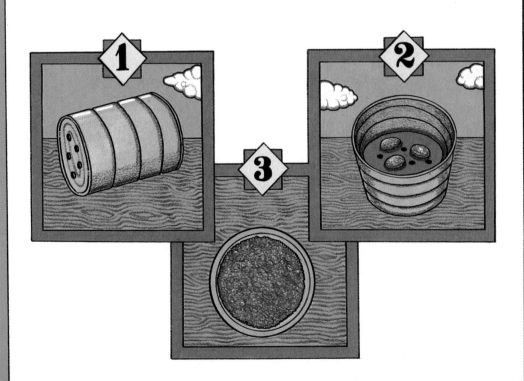

4. Dig three or four small holes
in the soil.
Drop a seed in each hole.
Pat some soil down over the seeds.

5. Water the soil with care.
Use a dish under the pot to catch
the water.
As you water it, look for the water
to drop from the holes in the end
of the pot.
When it starts to drop, the seeds
have all the water they need.

6. Put the pot and dish near
a window where there is sun.

7. Feel the soil each day.
If it is not wet, water it a bit.
Now it is time to wait.
The seeds will grow slowly.

8. After many days, you will see
small green plants in your pot.
Keep waiting and watering.
Before long, you will have flowers
that you helped to grow.

After You Read

Think

1. What was Grandma's idea for something to care for?

2. What do you think about before you try to grow a plant?

3. What is the best place for a plant that grows in a pot?

Share

How are pets and plants different?

Write

Write a sentence.
Tell why you think this story is called "City Magic."

Read

"A Garden for Miss Mouse," by Michaela Muntean, is another book about plants.

Farming

by Betty Baker

Coyote liked melons, all kinds
of melons.
But he did not have any.

Badger had a farm.
Coyote went to Badger and said,
"We are partners.
We should farm together."

"All right," said Badger.
"Help me dig."

"No," said Coyote.
"I am not good at digging.
You are.
You dig.
I will do the planting."

"No," said Badger.
"If you plant, you will make a mess.
I will dig and plant.
You pull the weeds."

Coyote said, "A partner should make things easy for you.
You live in a hole, so you take everything that grows under the ground.
I will just keep what grows on top."

"All right," said Badger, and he started to dig.
Coyote put his tail up and went away laughing.

When it was time to pull weeds,
Coyote was making a new song.
Badger pulled the weeds.

When it was time to pull them again,
Coyote was singing his new song to
the full moon.
Badger pulled the weeds.

Then Coyote went away to hunt
rabbits.

Badger pulled all the weeds.

When it was time to eat melons,
Coyote came back.
The plants were big and green.
But they had no melons.

"You took my melons!" said Coyote.
"You only get what grows under the
ground.
Give me my melons."

Badger said, "You did not tell
me you wanted melons.
I planted what I always plant."

"What is that?" said Coyote.

"Potatoes," said Badger.
And he dug them up and ate them
all winter.

Coyote said, "It is not right for
one partner to get everything."

Badger said, "It is not right
for one partner to do everything."

"You are right," said Coyote.
"You dig and plant.
I will pull the weeds.
And this time, I will take what
grows under the ground."

"All right," said Badger, and he
started to dig.
Coyote put his tail up and went away
laughing.

And he did not come back until
it was time to eat potatoes.
The plants were big and green.
Coyote dug and dug.
But the plants had no potatoes.
"Where are my potatoes?" said
Coyote.

Badger said, "You did not tell me
you wanted potatoes.
Last time, you wanted melons.
So that is what I planted."

And he dried the melons and ate
them all winter.

After You Read

Think

1. How did Coyote try to trick Badger?

2. How did Badger trick Coyote?

3. Why didn't Coyote help as he had promised?

Share

What are some good ways to get people to work with each other to get something done?

Write

Write two sentences.
Tell when it is good to make a promise.

Read

Another folktale about animals who play tricks is "The Banza" by Diane Wolkstein.

Have you ever looked at a star and thought about what it would be like to go to a new planet? In this story, a girl visits Earth and finds out the thing she likes best about it.

The Best New Thing

by Isaac Asimov

Rada lived on a little world, far out in space. Her father and her mother and her brother, Jonathan, lived there too.

Rada was the only little girl on the little world. Jonny was the only little boy. Rada's father and mother worked on the spaceships. They looked to see that everything was all right before the spaceships went on their way back to Earth or to other planets. Rada and Jonny would watch the ships come and go.

Rada and Jonny had to wear their space suits when they watched. There was no air on the little world, but inside their suits there was air and it was warm.

When people came out of the spaceships, they saw Rada and Jonny. One man said, "Would you like to see Earth someday?"

Jonny asked, "Are things different on Earth?"

"Well, the sky is blue," said the man.

"I have never seen a blue sky," said Rada.

"There is air on Earth. You don't have to wear a space suit," he said.

Rada said, "That must be nice. I will ask my father if I can go to Earth."

She jumped high to see where her father was. She jumped so high, she could see all around the spaceship. She did not see her father.

She pulled a little ring on her suit. That
made her go down again. She came down
very near the man.

The man said, "That is well done, but you
could not do that on Earth."

Rada said, "Why not?"

"On Earth," said the man, "you can only
jump a little way. Earth pulls you down right
away. And you roll down any slanting
place."

Then the man had to go into the spaceship
again. Rada and Jonny waited for their
father.

When their father came, Rada and Jonny went underground with him. Rada and Jonny and their father and mother lived inside the little world, in nice, large rooms.

Jonny said, "Dad, is it true that you don't have to wear a space suit on Earth?"

His father said, "Yes, it is. There is air on Earth."

Jonny said, "And is the sky really blue there?"

"That's right," his father answered. "And there are white things in the sky called clouds. Sometimes drops of water come from the sky. That is rain."

Rada thought about this, and then she said, "If the ground has water on it, don't people slip and fall?"

Her father laughed, and then he said, "The rain doesn't stay on top of the ground. It sinks into the ground and helps to make the grass grow."

"Will we go to Earth someday, Dad?"

"Yes, Rada," her father said. "Maybe we can go soon."

"Have I ever been there, Dad?" asked Rada.

"Yes," said her father. "You were born there, but you can't remember it because you were only a baby. And Jonny wasn't even born."

Rada and Jonny could not sleep that night. There were so many new things on Earth to think about. There was air that was everywhere. There were the blue sky and the rain, the wind and the flowers. And there were even birds and animals.

But there was one new thing Rada really wanted to do. She told Jonny about it and he wanted to do it, too. They didn't tell their father or mother. It was something they had never done before. On Earth, they were going to find out what it felt like.

One day a spaceship came and their father said, "This is the ship that will take us to Earth."

Rada felt a little bit sad. She would miss her little world. When they were getting into the spaceship, she turned and said, "I'm leaving now, little world. It is time for me to go to Earth. But I'll always remember you."

Then the spaceship started to move.

Rada could see the little world as the ship moved away from it. Soon it was just a dot, and then all Rada could see were the stars.

"Can we see Earth, Dad?" Jonny asked.

"It looks like a star from here. It's that bright one there," said his father.

"Look at Earth, Rada," said Jonny.

Rada looked at the bright star and was happy. Soon she would be on Earth and would know about the new thing. She knew Jonny was thinking about it, too.

When the ship stopped, Rada took off her belt. She was the first one to get out of the chair. Jonny was next.

"Aren't we going to put on our space suits?" asked Rada.

"Don't forget, we don't have to put on space suits on Earth," said her father.

"Yes," said Rada. "That's one of the new things." She and Jonny were waiting for another new thing, too. They held each other's hand, but they didn't say anything.

They all walked out of the ship. It was warm and the sun was very big.

"What is that sound?" asked Rada.

"It is a bird singing," said her mother.

Rada had never heard a bird singing. She had never felt the wind. She had never seen such a big sun and such bright sunlight.

These were all new things.

Now it was time for the best new thing of all.

She said, "Come on, Jonny."

Jonny said, "Look at the grass. And there's a little hill. Let's try it."

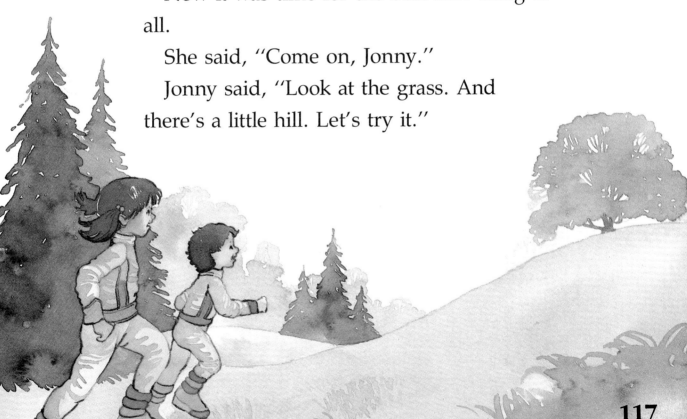

They ran to the little hill. Then they rolled down the hill. When they were done, they stood up, laughing.

Their father and mother came to them.

"You can't run like that here," said their mother.

"But we wanted to," said Rada. "We are so happy because we know, now, about the new thing."

"What new thing?" asked her father.

"We rolled down the hill," said Rada. "I think it's the best new thing of all."

"Yes," said Jonny. "It is!"

And they ran up to the top of the hill to try it again.

A Reader Says

I would like to visit Rada's home. I would like to go to a place where there's no gravity.

How did you feel about the story?

After You Read

Thinking About What You Read

1. How could Rada jump so high? Why did she pull a little ring to come down?

2. Why hadn't the children ever seen a blue sky, or birds?

3. How did Rada and Jonny feel about visiting Earth?

4. Why did the children laugh after they rolled down a hill?

Thinking About How You Read

Think about Rada in the end of the story. Things happen in order in a story. How did knowing that help you understand why Rada knew so little about Earth?

Sharing and Listening

Tell what you think Jonny and Rada liked and did not like about living in space. Listen as other children give their ideas.

Writing

Pretend you are going to Rada's world. Write a few sentences telling what would be the "best new thing" you would do there.

People have traveled to many places in outer space. But no one lives in space—yet. Have you ever thought about what it would be like to live in space?

The Newest Cities of All

by Judy Rosenbaum

People today live in some unusual places. There are towns on top of mountains. There are homes in dry deserts. Some people even live in houses under the ground.

Someday, we may live in even stranger places than these. We may have cities under the sea. We may put up homes at the South Pole. Or we may build towns in outer space.

We already fly into space. People have walked on our moon. Astronauts have spent weeks living in space. Right now, a space ship with no people in it is flying to the planet Pluto. One day, more people will travel in space. Some will go there to live. They will face some new problems.

120

Where in space would we build a city?
The moon looks like a good place. It is the
space body closest to Earth. We might also
try Mars. Mars is one of the nearest planets
to Earth. We could also build city-ships right
in space. These city-ships would never land.
They would just keep floating.

Many things will be the same about life in
space. We will still need to eat and sleep. We
will need and want to play, sing, tell stories,
and be with friends. We will not stop doing
these things just because we are in space.
But we may do some things in a new way.

Think about what is different in space.
There is no air in space or on other planets
we have found. There is no water. No plants
grow. People can't live without air or water.
They also need to grow food to eat.

How could we have air and water in
space? We would have to carry them along
with us in big tanks on the flight. We
already do this in spaceships. On a planet or
moon, we might build a big dome. This
dome would go over a city and keep the air
in. Maybe someday we will find a way to
make air and water from things in space.

Today, space travelers take special food along on spaceships. It is dried into little packs. But who would really want to live on dried food for a long time in a space city? It would be much better to grow food right near the city. We would have to take Earth plants along with us to plant there. We might not need to take soil with us, however. There is a new way to grow plants without soil. People can now put plants into water with special plant foods in it. Maybe this would be better than soil for growing plants in space. All that soil would be hard to carry in a spaceship. It would take up too much room in the ship, too.

Having to carry everything from Earth will be one of the biggest problems in space. There seems to be no life on the moon and most planets. All they have is rock. Rock can be used for building homes. But all other things will need to be flown in. This means *everything*—clothes, beds, glass for windows, even paper. People in space cities will need to take care of how they use things. They might find more ways to use things over and over and not throw them away. This is called *recycling*. Air will have to be recycled. So will some water. How could people recycle things like cloth and paper? How do we do this today on Earth?

People in space will want to talk to their friends on Earth. This will not be a big problem. We already know how to talk to each other across space. Do you remember seeing space flights on your TV screen? The astronauts talked to Earth. People on Earth could even watch on their TV screens astronauts moving around on the moon.

Maybe you will get to live in a space city one day. What do you think your life will be like? What will the streets look like? Will people ride bikes and skate down those streets? What kinds of clothes will people wear? What new machines will these cities hold? Will space cities look like the make-believe space cities you see on TV?

125

One day you may find out. You may even be one of the people who helps build such a city. One day, children may open a book a lot like this one. Inside will be a story about cities in space. And next to the story will be the face of someone living in that city—you.

A Reader Says

I would like to visit space, but I think I would miss Earth after a while.

How did you feel about the story?

After You Read

Thinking About What You Read

1. What would be the biggest problems with living in space?

2. Why would we have to find new ways to grow food?

3. Why would people in a space city use things over and over again?

4. Why might people someday live in space?

Thinking About How You Read

How did asking questions about cities in outer space help you find the facts?

Sharing and Listening

Tell why you think people might really live in space someday, or why not? Listen as other people give their ideas.

Writing

Write to a friend on Earth from your home in a space city. Tell what new things you have been doing.

Can an alligator talk? Read on to find out how some great creatures, such as alligators, talk to each other.

What Is That Alligator Saying?

by Ruth Belov Gross

People can tell each other things in a lot of different ways. They can do it by talking. And they can tell each other things without talking at all. They can use their hands. They can make faces. They can make funny sounds. They can cry.

Animals have ways of telling each other things, too. Sometimes we say they are talking to each other. But animals do not talk the way we do. They communicate in a special way.

Some animals do things that other animals can see. Some animals do things that other animals can feel. Some animals make sounds that other animals can hear. Some animals make smells other animals can smell.

Many kinds of baby animals cannot do things on their own. They need their mothers to feed them and to keep them safe.

These baby creatures have special ways to tell their mothers when they are hungry or in danger. And their mothers have special ways to warn the babies when there is danger.

Baby alligators communicate with their mothers by grunting. Whenever a mother alligator hears her babies grunting—*umph, umph, umph*—she comes to them right away.

The first time an alligator hears her babies, she is not able to see them. Their little grunts are coming from a bunch of old leaves and some mud. That is where the mother alligator laid her eggs many weeks before.

Now the mother alligator goes to the bunch of leaves. She digs it open with her long alligator snout. And there, under the leaves, are her babies! She helps them get out of their muddy nest.

If baby alligators couldn't communicate with their mother, what would happen? The mother alligator might forget to dig them out with her snout.

Mother alligators also communicate with their babies by grunting. *Umph, umph, umph*—a mother alligator is warning her babies that danger is near. The babies hide in the water when they hear this sound.

If a mother alligator couldn't warn her babies of danger, what would happen to them?

Animals cannot say "Watch out!" the way we can. They have their own ways of warning each other that danger may be near.

A beaver uses its tail to say "Watch out!" It brings its tail up over its back. Then it smacks its tail *hard* on the water of the beaver pond.

The sound can be heard far away. It tells other beavers that danger is near.

When the other beavers hear the smacking sound, they dive into the pond. But first they smack *their* tails on the water.

Smack! Whack! Smack! The beavers are passing the danger warning to other beavers around the pond.

Some birds make a lot of noise. Crows go *caw, caw, caw* a lot, and they make other noises, too.

Hubert Frings and his wife Mable Frings are two people who studied "crow talk." They wanted to find out how crows tell each other, "Watch out—danger! Fly away as fast as you can!" So they hid microphones near a bunch of crows.

After a while they had a lot of different crow sounds. Then they played the sounds back to the crows. They played the sounds one at a time.

They played the first sound back to the crows. Nothing happened. They played another sound, and again nothing happened.

Then they tried a third sound. When they played this sound, crows came flying from all over.

They tried one more crow sound—and this time all the crows flew away! The crows flew away every time that sound was played.

Now they knew which sound meant "watch out—fly away." They named this the "alarm call."

And they also knew which sound made the crows come together. They named this the "assembly call."

133

This story tells you some things about how animals communicate. But there is a lot more to know. If you want to, you can find out more by reading.

You can also find out more about how animals communicate by watching what animals do. You can watch flies and ants, and you can watch cats and birds.

Maybe you will find out something that no one knew before.

A Reader Says

I never knew that the sounds animals made were more than just noise!

How did you feel about the story?

After You Read

Thinking About What You Read

1. What are some ways animals can talk to each other?
2. Why do beavers smack their tails in place of using their voices?
3. How did the Frings know that they understood what the crows were saying?
4. Why do animals communicate with each other?

Thinking About How You Read

How did asking yourself what the story was about help you understand it?

Sharing and Listening

Tell which facts you liked the most in this story. Which animals would you like to know more about? Listen as others tell what they liked the most.

Writing

Write the ways that alligators, crows, and beavers talk. Then write about other animals you know and the ways they might communicate.

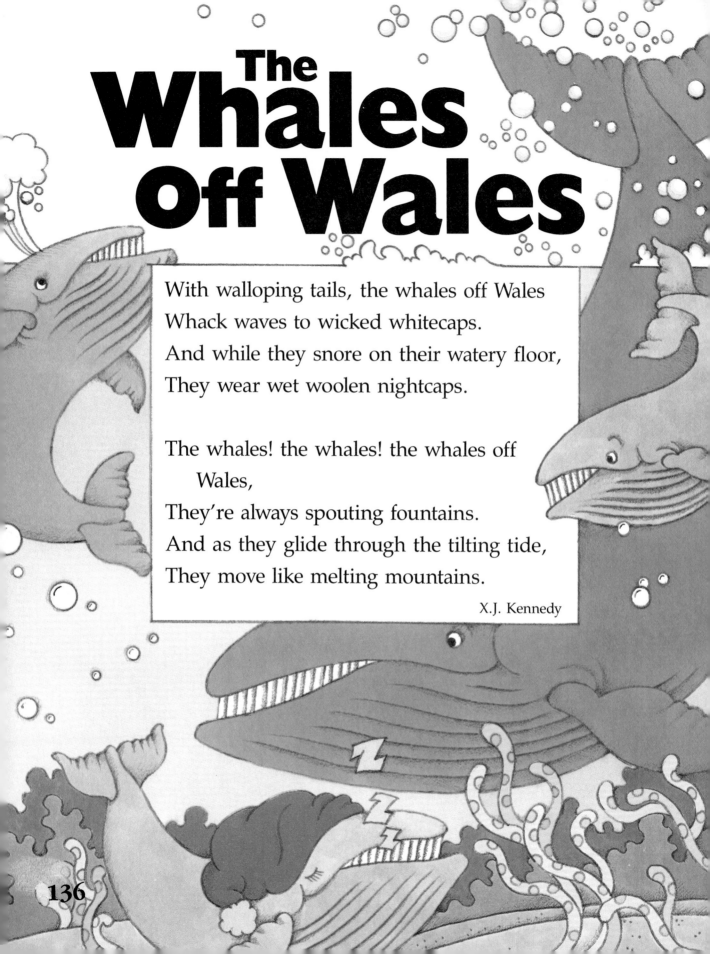

The Whales Off Wales

With walloping tails, the whales off Wales
Whack waves to wicked whitecaps.
And while they snore on their watery floor,
They wear wet woolen nightcaps.

The whales! the whales! the whales off
    Wales,
They're always spouting fountains.
And as they glide through the tilting tide,
They move like melting mountains.

X.J. Kennedy

After You Read

Thinking About What You Read

1. What are the largest creatures that are alive today?

2. What does the poet say the whales do with their tails? What do you think this means?

3. What do you think the poet means by "woolen nightcaps"?

4. Why do you think the poet describes whales as "Spouting fountains" and moving as "melting mountains"?

Thinking About How You Read

How did the details the poet used to describe the whales help you understand the poet's main idea of the poem?

Sharing and Listening

Which part of the poem did you like best? Share your ideas. Listen as others give their ideas.

Writing

Think about another large animal. Write a sentence about it. Use words to describe it that repeat the same sounds.

To mice, a cat can seem a great, big, scary
creature. In this play based on a fable by
Aesop, some mice want to save their town
from a cat. What can they do?

Belling the Cat

by Laura Schenone

CAST

AESOP	RANDOLPH
JOAN	CHARLES
THE MAYOR	JENNY
BERNARD	BETH

AESOP: Once there was a small town where many mice made their home. It was a very nice town for mice. There were schools and stores and a baseball team. There was even a mayor to help the mice run the town. One morning the mayor wakes up to the sound of knocking. She runs to see who it is.

MAYOR: Who in the world could be in such a hurry to see me? Joan! What has happened?

JOAN: The Cat just chased me clear across the field. I was nibbling on some nuts when I saw The Cat. Mayor, you have to do something. It's impossible to be safe from The Cat!

MAYOR: (*sighing*) I know. I just had a close call myself. The other day I was walking to the City Hole and The Cat came out of nowhere. I had to dive under some leaves.

JOAN: Mayor, this can't go on. We are all living in fear. The Cat is everywhere, and it's your job to do something!

MAYOR: Tell all the mice to come to the Town Meeting Hole tonight. We'll take care of this cat once and for all.

DOWN WITH CATS!

NO CATS!

OUR WONDERFUL MAYOR!

MAYOR

TOWN MEETING TONIGHT! ABOUT THE CAT!!

AESOP: The news travels fast.
Every mouse is at the Town
Meeting Hole that night. All of them
are talking at once. The air buzzes with
stories of close calls with The Cat.

MAYOR: Friends, I will not waste your time
with a long speech. We are here to
talk about a big problem. Tonight, we
must face the thing that makes us live
in fear. We must do something about
our number one problem . . . The Cat.

ALL OF THE MICE: Boo! Hiss! Boo!

CHARLES: It's easy to boo. The hard part is
to think of what to do.

MAYOR: Charles is right! We need a plan.
Does anyone have an idea to suggest?

BERNARD: I do! I suggest we move!

ALL OF THE MICE: Move??!!

BERNARD: Yes, move. The Cat never leaves this field. I know a pretty spot where The Cat never goes. There is a flower bed at the end of the field.

JENNY: Where is this place?

BERNARD: It is on the other side of the wall.

MAYOR: How do you get there?

BERNARD: Go to the big hole under the wall. Turn right. Follow the old road for fifty feet to a large field. Turn left when you see a piece of paper that reads "WATCH OUT—MOUSETRAP AHEAD." Keep walking. At the end of the field is a nice pond. We could build a new town next to the pond. Then we would be safe.

CHARLES: What, Bernard? Run? That doesn't sound like fun. *This* is the best field around. We must stay here and stand our ground!

MAYOR: Charles is right again. We need a better plan.

JENNY: (*whispering*) Maybe we're too noisy. If we can be more quiet, then The Cat will not be able to find us. We will never have to run from him again.

CHARLES: Jenny, your plan is very nice, but we are already as quiet as mice. The Cat is so sly, he never says meow. He may even be listening to us now! (*All the mice in the Town Meeting Hole look around them in fear of The Cat.*)

ALL OF THE MICE: Oh what will we do!

RANDOLPH: I have it! I know what we might
do. We can meet with The Cat and
talk things over. Maybe we could get
him to see our side. Maybe we could
get him to leave us alone.

CHARLES: Randolph, that's a very nice wish,
but we might as well jump into The
Cat's food dish. We can no longer
pretend that The Cat is our friend.

MAYOR: (*sighing*) Once again you're right,
Charles. Talking to The Cat would be
impossible. But there must be
something we can do. Doesn't anyone
else have an idea?

CHARLES: Well, mayor, I do. Let me tell it
to you.

AESOP: All of the mice get very quiet so they can hear every word.

CHARLES: Mayor, The Cat always finds us because he is so sly and quiet. I have a plan and I think we might try it. We need something, it is clear, that will let us know when he is near. If The Cat would make noise, he would never find us. We could all run away when we heard him behind us. Let's get a bell and a little bit of string. We will put it around his neck and be able to hear it ring.

AESOP: The mice cheer and clap. They are very happy. It is the best idea they have ever heard. Soon they can be rid of The Cat. Then, Beth, the oldest, smartest mouse of all stands up and speaks in a mild voice.

BETH: I like that idea, Charles. Now I know why all the mice look up to you. But I have just one thing to ask. I think you know what I'm getting at. . . . Who will be the mouse to put the bell on The Cat?

AESOP: It is easy to suggest impossible solutions.

A Reader Says

I thought Bernard's idea was the best. All the mice could move and build a new town. Then they'd be safe.

How did you feel about the play?

After You Read

Thinking About What You Read

1. What is so special about the mice in this play?

2. Why were so many mice afraid of one cat?

3. What might have happened if the mice had tried to carry out Bernard's plan?

4. How might Charles have answered if another mouse had suggested putting a bell on the cat?

Thinking About How You Read

How did knowing the mice would learn something help you understand the ending of the fable?

Sharing and Listening

Think about how the mice in this play escaped the cat. Remember how the animals in "What Is That Alligator Saying?" escaped danger. Compare the animals' problems. Tell how they are the same or different. Listen as other people share their ideas.

Writing

Pretend you are a mouse. Write a story about how the cat scared you. Tell how you would make the cat leave.

Alexander, a live mouse, wishes he could be more like his friend Willy, who is a toy mouse. But Alexander learns that sometimes what you wish for isn't what is best.

Alexander and the Wind-up Mouse

by Leo Lionni

"Help! Help! A mouse!" There was a scream. Then a crash. Cups, saucers, and spoons were flying in all directions.

Alexander ran for his hole as fast as his little legs would carry him.

All Alexander wanted was a few crumbs, and yet every time they saw him they would scream for help or chase him with a broom.

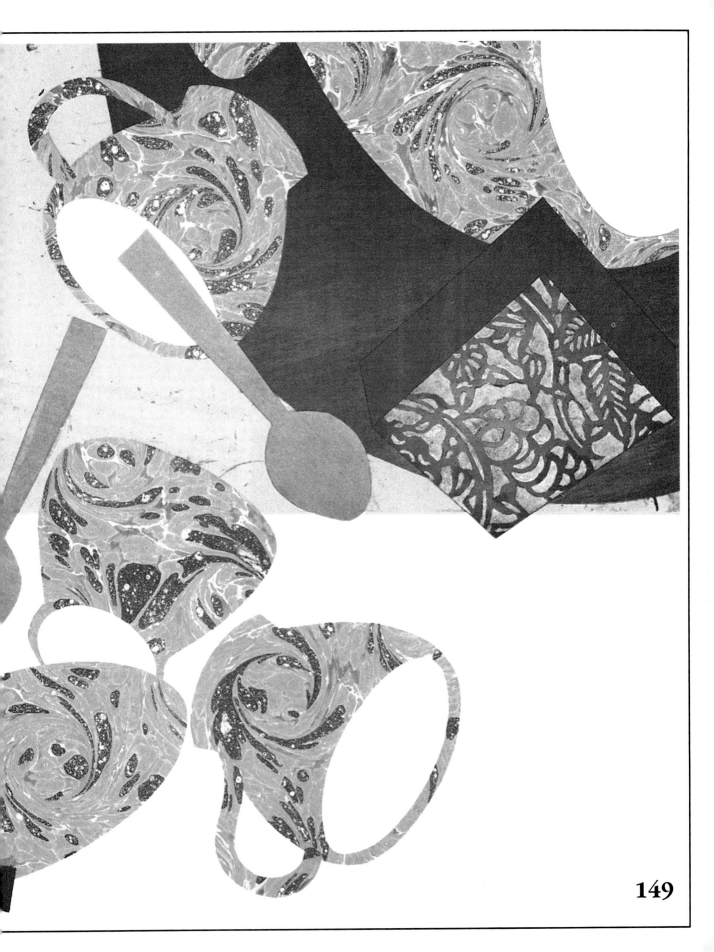

One day, when there was no one in the house, Alexander heard a squeak in Annie's room. He sneaked in and what did he see? Another mouse.

But not an ordinary mouse like himself. Instead of legs it had two little wheels, and on its back there was a key.

"Who are you?" asked Alexander.

"I am Willy the wind-up mouse, Annie's favorite toy. They wind me to make me run around in circles, they cuddle me, and at night I sleep on a soft white pillow between the doll and a woolly teddy bear. Everyone loves me."

"They don't care much for me," said Alexander sadly. But he was happy to have found a friend. "Let's go to the kitchen and look for crumbs," he said.

"Oh, I can't," said Willy. "I can only move when they wind me. But I don't mind. Everybody loves me."

Alexander, too, came to love Willy. He
went to visit him whenever he could. He told
him of his adventures with brooms, flying
saucers, and mousetraps. Willy talked about
the penguin, the woolly bear, and mostly
about Annie. The two friends spent many
happy hours together.

152

But when he was alone in the dark of his hideout, Alexander thought of Willy with envy.

"Ah!" he sighed. "Why can't I be a wind-up mouse like Willy and be cuddled and loved?"

One day Willy told a strange story. "I've heard," he whispered mysteriously, "that in the garden, at the end of the pebble path, close to the blackberry bush, there lives a magic lizard who can change one animal into another."

"Do you mean," said Alexander, "that he could change me into a wind-up mouse like you?"

That very afternoon Alexander went into the garden and ran to the end of the path. "Lizard, lizard," he whispered. And suddenly there stood before him, full of the colors of flowers and butterflies, a large lizard. "Is it true that you could change me into a wind-up mouse?" asked Alexander in a quivering voice.

"When the moon is round," said the lizard, "bring me a purple pebble."

For days and days Alexander searched the garden for a purple pebble. In vain. He found yellow pebbles and blue pebbles and green pebbles—but not one tiny purple pebble.

At last, tired and hungry, he returned to the house. In a corner of the pantry he saw a box full of old toys, and there, between blocks and broken dolls, was Willy. "What happened?" said Alexander, surprised.

Willy told him a sad story. It had been Annie's birthday. There had been a party and everyone had brought a gift. "The next day," Willy sighed, "many of the old toys were dumped in this box. We will all be thrown away."

Alexander was almost in tears. "Poor, poor Willy!" he thought. But then suddenly something caught his eye. Could it really be . . .? Yes it was! It was a little purple pebble.

157

All excited, he ran to the garden, the precious pebble tight in his arms. There was a full moon. Out of breath, Alexander stopped near the blackberry bush. "Lizard, lizard, in the bush," he called quickly. The leaves rustled and there stood the lizard. "The moon is round, the pebble found," said the lizard. "Who or what do you wish to be?"

"I want to be . . ." Alexander stopped. Then suddenly he said, "Lizard, lizard, could you change Willy into a mouse like me?" The lizard blinked. There was a blinding light. And then all was quiet. The purple pebble was gone.

Alexander ran back to the house as fast as he could.

The box was there, but alas it was empty. "Too late," he thought, and with a heavy heart he went to his hole in the baseboard.

Something squeaked! Cautiously Alexander moved closer to the hole. There was a mouse inside. "Who are you?" said Alexander, a little frightened.

"My name is Willy," said the mouse.

"Willy!" cried Alexander. "The
lizard . . . the lizard did it!" He hugged
Willy and then they ran to the garden path.
And there they danced until dawn.

A Reader Says

I think it's more fun to be real than to be a toy.

How did you feel about the story?

After You Read

Thinking About What You Read

1. Why did Alexander wish he was a wind-up mouse like Willy?

2. Why did Alexander change his mind about wanting to be a toy mouse?

3. What do you think Alexander thought when he found the box empty?

4. What do you think Alexander and Willy will do together now that Willy is no longer a toy mouse?

Thinking About How You Read

What details of the story make it seem make-believe?

Sharing and Listening

Tell why you think both Alexander and Willy will be happy now. Listen as others share their ideas.

Writing

Make believe you are Willy or Alexander. Think about what you would like to do together. Write a list of things to do.

About the Author

Leo Lionni

Leo Lionni was born in Amsterdam, Holland. When he was 29 years old, he came to live in the United States. Before writing books, he painted. His paintings have been shown in museums.

Mr. Lionni does all the drawings for his books. Some of his other books are *The Biggest House in the World*, *Frederick*, and *Geraldine, The Music Mouse*. Mr. Lionni has won many prizes for his books.

Mr. Lionni once said that he wrote for the child in himself who has never grown up. That way, he hopes, the child in every person can enjoy his books.

165